Keep your Promise

To: Mikayla, Alicia and Abby

"Always be honest and
hold true to your word"

During a beautiful morning on the beach, Mrs. Crab walked with her son Paco. She told him the importance of knowing how to swim. And the dangers he could face if he did not listen to the advice of his parents.

"Son, I know you are learning to swim and you will be an expert like your father."

"Mom, I know how to move my legs fast in the water. I can jump off the big rock now, like my dad and his friends do."

"Son, to jump off the big rock, you must do more than move your legs quickly; It takes much time to practice as well. And you are just a little crab, you need to grow and become stronger."

"Promise you will never jump from the big rock until you grow up son, you will be able to do these things one day."

"How long will it take to grow up?" Paco said.

"Son, time flies and when you least expect it, you will be as strong as your father."

"I promise mom, I will wait until I am ready."

Satisfied by the promise of her son, Mrs. Crab decided to go home and rest for a while.

Paco decided to approach the big rock and watch how adult crabs jumped into the sea. He watched intently and thought: "I am still very young, but soon I will grow up and I will jump from the top of the big rock and I will swim to the bottom of the sea like my dad."

Upon arriving home he ate dinner with his parents, they all said, "good night" and everyone went to bed. That night the little crab awoke while everyone was sleeping, he had an idea. "This is the perfect time to jump off the big rock at sea, everyone is asleep and no one will be able to see me."

Leaving the house, he ran to the beach, forgetting the promise he had made to his Mom. When he came to the big rock, he climbed, reached the top and said: "This is very easy; all I have to do is close my eyes, jump and swim!"

Without hesitation, Paco leaped into the ocean. When he hit the water, Paco moved his legs, not knowing which way he was swimming with closed eyes. "I have to keep moving fast to reach the shore soon."

A turtle passed by and noticed Paco swimming in circles. "I have to help him, before the big waves take him to sea," the turtle thought to himself.

"I think I'm about to reach the shore,
because I've been swimming a long time."

The turtle put the little crab on the sand. Immediately, Paco opened his eyes. He started jumping and he yelled: "I did it, I did it!"

"No, little crab, what you did was very dangerous, you could have had a bad accident." Since your eyes were closed, you did not realize that I was the one who brought you out of the water."

"Son, what are you doing here?"

"I found him swimming close to the big rock,"
replied the turtle. "Fortunately, I was able to
get him and move him to the shore safety,
just in time before the big waves."

Paco's parents thanked Mr. Turtle, for helping their son and then returned home with the little crab.

Then, Dad said: "Paco, you promised your mom, not to jump from the big rock." "We are very disappointed son, you have to obey your parents and keep your promises. You did not obey. Now, nobody will believe you."

"I'm sorry for not keeping my promise, please forgive me."

One week later...

Six months later...

The big day has come.

Finally, Paco's Mom
and Dad granted him
permission to jump
from the big rock. That day was
very happy for everyone, especially
because Paco had kept his promise
to wait to be an adult.

He finally swam like his Dad.

"I did it at last! Paco said."

Honor your father and your mother, so that you may live long in the land the Lord your God is giving you.

Exodus 20:12

Paco the Crab

Paco the Crab is an only child. He was born in northern Colombia on the Rosario Islands where some communities of blue crabs live. His parents are dedicated to the education of their son. His Crab family has always instilled the values of obedience, diligence and discipline. Paco became known as a young champion in free diving from the big rock. He began his athletic training at an early age. With dedication and commitment, Paco today is one of the best divers on the island. Paco achieved speed, agility and dexterity with his athletic pursuits. He continues living on his native island and serves as a diving coach for the new generations.

Sandra Padilla Malkus began her career as a physical therapist in the country of Colombia. She has always had a passion for writing children's books and enjoys the fascinating publishing world. Sandra is a community volunteer for organizations including the Colombian Volunteer Ladies and Extending a Hand. She lives in Fort Lauderdale with her husband Chuck and Troy, a four-legged family member.

Chuck Malkus is an author and keynote speaker who enjoys sharing lessons about life choices. A charismatic storyteller, he shares personal experiences that reveal the unexpected returns of giving back and the importance of strong values. Chuck co-founded Neighbors 4 Neighbors in 1992 and has served as a board of director for numerous non-profit organizations.

Eliane Guzman, originally from Ecuador, has always enjoyed making a difference in the communities where she lives. Her passion for design and art began when she was a youngster. Today, in addition to illustrating children's books, she cherishes spending time with her husband David and daughter Abby. One of the things Eliane enjoys about living in South Florida is the number of art shows taking place on weekends.

Promises to Keep

....

....

....

....

....

....

....

....

....

....

....

Made in the USA
Coppell, TX
20 January 2022

72009736R00021